THE ONLINE MEETINGS HANDBOOK

Also by Gary Genard

How to Give a Speech
Easy-to-Learn Skills for Successful Presentations,
Speeches, Pitches, Lectures, and More!

Fearless Speaking
Beat Your Anxiety, Build Your Confidence,
Change Your Life

THE ONLINE MEETINGS HANDBOOK

THE NEW RULES FOR PERSONAL AND TEAM SUCCESS

GARY GENARD

Cedar &
Maitland
Press

To order this book, please call (617) 993-3410, or
contact info@genardmethod.com. Group and academic
discounts are available.

The Genard Method
93 Concord Avenue, Suite 3
Belmont, MA 02478
www.genardmethod.com
info@genardmethod.com
(617) 993-3410

Twitter: @GaryGenard
LinkedIn: www.linkedin.com/in/garygenard

ISBN: 978-0-9796314-3-6

Library of Congress Control Number: 2020923814

Printed in the United States of America

Dedicated to my clients

"If you really want to learn something, teach it." — An old saying

TABLE OF CONTENTS

Introduction

The Key to Succeeding in Online Meetings

How good are you at selling your ideas online?

What about selling yourself and your company?

When you speak professionally, you have just one task: to communicate effectively with listeners who matter. If you're finding that's more of a challenge in video conferences, you're not alone.

The Online Meetings Handbook is a manual for connecting with and influencing others in the virtual environment. Whatever your job is, right now that goal is as important as anything else you achieve.

The question becomes, then: Are you and your team performing at 100% of your capabilities in online meetings? If not, this book is for you.

Your company has probably been using virtual technology for some time. After all, PictureTel Corp., known for its early video conferencing technology, produced significant sales starting in 1987.[1]

But Covid-19 changed the rules, seemingly overnight—and we found ourselves on a rocket ship bound for the virtual universe. Interacting largely or completely online hasn't only brought challenges and opportunities. It has actually changed the way we do business.

Suddenly, the world has been reduced

---

[1] https://en.wikipedia.org/wiki/PictureTel_Corp.

to the size of a small screen. To command that screen and positively influence others, you need a new *virtual persona*. And there's been no time or training to help you develop one.

That's what this book is all about. It offers specific *performance-based techniques* you won't find anywhere else, backed up by my two decades of helping people speak to influence. These approaches will a) help you look and sound at your virtual best, b) improve your presentation skills and on-camera effectiveness, and c) strengthen your overall online presence.

These approaches work equally well for you as an individual and for your team. They had better do so—because the need to succeed in online meetings is truly "virtually" the same for you and your colleagues and customers.

This is the way we communicate now.

Are you ready to speak at your best by learning the new rules?

Get Good at Online Meetings . . . Right Away!

Online business meetings have become a way of life. So, you'd better get good at video conferences . . . right away!

There has certainly been a learning curve in terms of the virtual, screen-based platforms we're now performing on. Online meetings and conferences have become the lifeblood of many of our businesses. And that has resulted in scrambling, hits-and-misses for individuals and teams, and generally having to adjust our thinking and expectations.

But aside from technology, what about the performance aspects of all of this? That should be front and center in all of our minds in our efforts to become more effective online communicators.

Why Your Video Skills Matter Now

If the shutdowns we're all experiencing had been short-lived, this wouldn't be as important a matter as it actually is. We would have experienced some awkwardness in adapting on the fly, then returned to our normal way of doing business.

But that's not what's happening. It isn't just team meetings and brainstorming sessions that are on our agendas now. It's pitches and sales presentations, webinars, gaining buy-in for our plans within our organization, and disseminating ideas across companies and industries. It's international panels and conferences. It is, in fact, all kinds of communication among small or large groups. The virtual stage is now a more essential space than ever. And we'd better learn how to use it to our advantage and those we speak to.

Interestingly, there's actually a huge and unseen advantage to improving our skills in front of a webcam. It's one that I think hasn't been recognized sufficiently: when we rehearse now, we're preparing in the actual venue we'll be speaking in.

That "we" actually means you, and your next online meeting.

The venue now isn't your company's conference room or your customer's facility. It's your webcam and cyberspace. Rehearsing (and improving your skills) in your office or home never had that advantage before, since you'd eventually be speaking in another location. But now, any improvement in your online communication skills gets fed directly into the finished product: your performance in a virtual meeting. What you see and hear when you record your practice for a video conference, for instance, is exactly what your fellow participants will experience.

That's why you need to get really good at it. Below is one way in particular you can do that.

How to Prepare and Practice an Online Presentation

One powerful tool you can use is the screen-recording feature of your platform. In Zoom (the software I use), screen recording is effortless; and it's just as valuable as videotaping in face-to-face interactions. Come to think of it, "face-to-face" is an appropriate term for video-based meetings as well.

Here is how I suggest you put your talks together to go from good to great as an online presenter. Start speaking out loud as early in the process as possible. Don't spend too much time in the "literary" realm by writing notes then editing and polishing them.

As soon as your purpose for this presentation is clear in your mind, start speaking what you might actually say, because the oral arena is where you'll be strutting your stuff. Importantly, only write down what sounds "right" in terms of how you want to reach your listeners at this point.

By the time you've assembled your first draft, you'll be very close to the speech you want to make to this audience. That's a much better outcome than some rough notes that may or may not be on the mark when you actually start talking about them.

At this point, it's time to practice and record yourself in front of your webcam. As I mentioned above, when you watch yourself afterwards you'll see and hear exactly what everyone else will be experiencing. You couldn't buy that level of accuracy before now unless you had planned for a video meeting in the first place.

Think of it as a silver lining in this age of enforced video conferencing.

2

The Best 'Tips and Tricks' for Starting a Meeting

How can you provide high energy if it's your team's sixth video conference of the day? Here are the best tips and tricks for starting an online meeting.

"The show must go on."

How many times have you heard those words? According to the Cambridge Idioms Dictionary, that's "a phrase used to convey the idea that an event or activity must continue even if there are problems or difficulties, with or without regard to actual show business."[2]

Video conferences certainly aren't show business. But if they matter to you personally, and to your company's success (and they do) ... well, the show must go on. It doesn't matter that all of you have been in front of your screens for hours and barely have enough energy left to sit up straight.

If you were in the theater, right about now the stage manager would be rapping on the dressing room door. "Five minutes!" he or she would announce. And you'd put aside everything else that's in your mind and throw yourself into the performance.

What's the difference between that and performing well in a virtual meeting? Not as much as you might think! So, where do you get the energy? Let's talk about that.

---

[2] Cambridge Idioms Dictionary (Cambridge: Cambridge University Press, 2006). https://en.wikipedia.org/wiki/The_show_must_go_on.

Developing a Performance Mindset

The place you need to start is not in your body, but in your head. Recently, for instance, a client said to me: "You're always the same in our online meetings. You always have the exact same level of energy, no matter what's happened to you that day."

Well, I hadn't really thought about it; but I did at that moment. And I realized the answer was that, for most of my life I've been a professional performer.

For performers, "the show must go on" never needs to be stated. It's simply understood. You have to give your 500th performance in *Hamilton* tonight and you didn't sleep much last night? Too bad. You have exactly the same responsibility to tonight's paying customers that you had on opening night.

This isn't to suggest that actors are more noble human beings than, say, business professionals. It's just that they understand a simple fact: performances need a higher level of energy than everyday interactions. So you just gather yourself, find the energy, and do it.

Here's a thought that should provide focus for you: In every situation where you interact with other people, you're performing . . . online meetings included! You might say it's your fiduciary duty (and that of every team member) to give 100% of whatever you've got left to the discussion. Truly, your company and its stakeholders are depending upon all of you to do so.

How to Manufacture 'Performance Rocket Fuel'

Where do you find this energy? Pretty close to home: in your own body. Once you have a performance mindset going for you, you only need to develop some breathing habits combined with movement to rev up your engines.

The truth is, you won't feel sufficiently energized if you're not breathing properly—and unfortunately, too few of us do that when it comes to public speaking. Add to that the lethargy that comes from sitting indoors for long periods without any physical activity, and it's no wonder you run out of gas.

If you can, take five minutes and practice any exercise that will help focus you and get more oxygen in your system. (One of the easiest ways to do that is just take a short stroll out of doors.) In these days of frazzled attention spans after endless meetings, anything that will steady and focus you is well worth a few minutes. If possible, try to add some movement to these moments of refreshing yourself.

Why Move? Physical movement requires oxygen, so this is another way to kick-start yourself into a more active mood. That includes your mental state.

Your brain needs the oxygen increase to help you think on your feet . . . or on your seat in this case. And there's nothing like even a modest amount of exercise to clear away those video-cobwebs.

And feel free to encourage the team members to do so on their own, between meetings. If everyone joins the meeting in a more refreshed state, so much the better.

Time to Get Creative in Your Next Online Meeting

If you're the host, and your body and brain have been re-oxygenated and reenergized this way, you can get creative about how to start meetings with more pep and pizzazz. Here are some ideas:

• Go with something other than "Hi, hello . . . how are you?" Even "What's new?" isn't going to elicit much, since everyone has been stuck at home in front of a screen since what seems like the beginning of time.

What could be new? Instead, use some of the same greetings, questions, or chit-chat that people used to use in the office.

• Set a rule: Whoever is hosting the meeting has to start off with an unusual fact.

• Or the host has to share something from their own life, and everyone has to say whether they think it's true or made up.

• Make a rule that the first five or ten minutes are chat-time, before the team gets down to business. Especially if everyone is in back-to-back meetings, this is decompression time. It may even get people to actually look forward to (at least the beginning of) the meeting.

• Use virtual backgrounds. The pro version of Zoom allows you to use photographs or video clips. Some of them are really fun and may wake people up. If you go with a video clip, choose one that doesn't have so much visual movement that it's distracting.

- Be on the lookout for visuals you can share with the attendees. Or even consider using the occasional slide to break up your part of the discussion. We all respond strongly to visuals, and one reason meetings drag is because they are all discussion and there's nothing interesting to look at.

- Use storytelling. We respond just as strongly to stories as we do to visuals. Don't tell shaggy dog tales. But incorporate a personal anecdote, a customer experience, or something the team would appreciate hearing about.

- Remember, stories don't have to be formal affairs that you've carefully rehearsed. Even mentioning what someone did, in this situation, and what happened because of it, will do the trick. And always, find a way to weave the data into a story where human beings are front-and-center.

3

How Your Team Can Look and Sound at Their Best

Is your team struggling to speak comfortably and successfully in virtual settings? Do they broadcast presence and confidence? Here's how they can look and sound at their best!

I just finished an intriguing book, a literary analysis of Edgar Allan Poe's writing by the late professor and poet Daniel Hoffman.

The book is titled *Poe Poe Poe Poe Poe Poe Poe*. It's a reference to Poe's famous poem, "The Bells":

Of the bells, bells, bells, bells,

Bells, bells, bells—

To the rhyming and the chiming of the bells!

So? Well, the book's title put me in mind of what for some of us is the make-up of our lives these days:

Zoom Zoom Zoom Zoom Zoom Zoom Zoom!

It certainly isn't the way we imagined embracing virtual communication more, is it? Whether you're hearing imaginary bells yourself by now, or just suffering from garden-variety Zoom fatigue, it pays to ask an important question. That goes for every member of your team. (So make sure everybody reads this!) The question is:

"How can I look and sound at my best in the virtual environment?"

Are You Talking to a Man or a Mouse?

First, let's discuss what the other participants in your online meetings are seeing. We should do so because, as always, visuals are important concerning how your audience perceives and judges you and your fellow team members. And that starts with your setup.

How do you feel these days about the army of virtual speakers you've seen who seem to be talking to a mouse? That's because they position their screen on their desk or tabletop so they're talking down to it.

Why is this still happening? Aside from being a horrible angle for anyone to view your face, it just doesn't look professional.

Whether you're on a laptop, tablet, or smartphone, you should use a stand so that your webcam is 2-3" below eye level (mine is set at 2½").

In addition, position your device so it's about 2 feet away from you. That way, viewers can see some of your gestures. This helps keep up everyone's attention level; and of course, gestures emphasize and clarify what you're saying.

If you choose to stand while presenting (which is perfectly fine), then of course you'll need to be farther away from the screen. And if this is your preferred presentation mode, I suggest getting a good wireless lapel microphone so the sound quality is right.

Finally, set up a light source in front of you so it shines on your face. This can be anything from a ring light of the type used to shoot YouTube videos, to a lamp with an ordinary 60-watt bulb. As long as it allows for illumination and is positioned correctly, your face will go from a death-like grayish hue to lifelike flesh tones. Welcome back to the living!

Can I Hear You Now? Yes, I Can.

What about microphones when you're sitting, Air Pods, or headsets to enhance the experience? Some of my clients use them and some don't. I've tried using an external microphone in online meetings, as well as wired and wireless headphones, and I don't think any of it is necessary for the average individual or team Zoom meeting.

First, your laptop is designed for this type of interaction, and the goods are already in the package. A laptop's built-in mic works perfectly well, for instance, in picking up the human voice—especially since you're sitting so close to it. And phones, of course, are made for speaking. If on the other hand you're recording podcasts or YouTube videos and you need professional quality in terms of voice reproduction, then go for the expensive microphone.

In terms of what you hear, i.e., internal speakers versus a headset, the former should be fine. That's because conversation uses a far narrower range of frequencies than, say, orchestral music. (One reason I don't like using a phone for virtual meetings is that the sound is below par in terms of human resonances.)

And there's this: one of the strengths of Zoom calls is the intimacy they can foster, even though the participants may be thousands of miles apart. Again, that's because you're very close to the device that is transmitting you elsewhere digitally. The more natural you look, the easier that communication is facilitated. It can be off-putting to have a conversation with someone wearing earphones!

GARY GENARD

Go Ahead . . . Have a Conversation

That word is key to looking and sounding your best in virtual engagements: conversation. The more you and every team member think that that's what you're doing—rather than giving a presentation— the more natural and effective you'll be.

It may be difficult for you to imagine the difference between the sound of someone delivering data, versus sharing that information with the listener. With some of my clients—including, for instance, CEOs and CFOs in earnings calls—we spend significant time moving from the former to the latter. A good speech coach will be able to demonstrate the difference out loud, using exactly the same spoken content. (This is a huge reason why I recommend finding a virtual speech coach who is also an actor.)

As a shortcut to being conversational: focus on *why* as much as *what*. That is, remind yourself of why you need to get this information across to these folks.

The information may be important; but your listeners are far more so. Put all of your focus and energy into getting them to understand this topic, idea, etc. You'll be surprised at how much more present you sound.

In fact, not virtual at all.

4

Make Your Online Meetings More Enjoyable and Productive

Working remotely has rapidly taken over important sectors of the economy. Has your business given serious thought to how to improve your virtual engagements?

When the coronavirus took hold in the U.S. in March 2020 and the lockdowns began, our nation felt like it was in free fall. Some segments of the economy were lucky enough, however, to switch employees from working in the office to doing so remotely, and were able to survive. In some cases, they have thrived. But in almost all instances, the change was disruptive.

Still, we persevered. But what was once an emergency response has become the norm—at least for certain types of businesses. Today, sixty-four percent of U.S. employees are working from home. And communication remains as important as ever. According to the Graduate Management Admissions Council, four of the most important skills that employers mention are communication-related: oral communication, listening skills, written communication, and presentation skills.[3]

Clearly, it's time to turn our attention from adapting to the world of webcasts, to learning how to excel in it. Following are some ways to make your online meetings more enjoyable and productive.

---

[3] "The New Skills Gap," Quantified Communications, October 2020 Newsletter.

To begin: if you're still thinking mostly in terms of adapting past practices to remote meetings, it's time to change your mindset. Virtual meetings and conferences are the reality. You should be looking for ways to make them engaging and exciting experiences for your company and its customers and clients.

Virtual Meetings Are Different. Make Them More So.

• Set the right tone for the event. Everyone expects the same old reality of "another Zoom meeting." Instead, provide them with above-the-ordinary levels of energy, focus, organization, and clarity of purpose. If you'd prefer the virtual engagement to have a light touch, make that apparent in the invitation or at the start.

• Use the first 5-10 minutes to allow everyone to decompress from the meeting they just left. Call it "Decompression

Time" and set it up so people share things that wouldn't otherwise be included in the meeting. This is actually a productive way to get down to business.

• Be creative in this segment. Consider virtual icebreakers, including games (some may take a bit longer than 10 minutes). You'll find lots of free sites for these tools!

• Make the meeting human. Ask everyone to bring a photo of a family pet, or a childhood or high-school graduation photo.

• There are online tools and software for brainstorming, collaboration, and decision-making if these are goals for the meeting.

• Use polls. These are great tools for understanding participants' knowledge and needs. They are also valuable in gauging people's energy level, whether the team should take a break, etc. You can write polling questions out beforehand, or even compose them in the meeting itself.

- Try breakout rooms. Set up separate sessions with sub-groups that can benefit from discussing issues on their own, then reporting back. Just a break from the regular routine of a huge overall meeting can be helpful.

- Give regular feedback during the session. It's far too easy for virtual meeting participants to feel like they're floating in cyberspace without an anchor.

- If you're conducting a webinar, there are many tools to help ramp up the feedback mechanism. In Zoom, for instance, there is the Q & A tool, and hand raising to bring up questions. You can enlist panelists, who can conduct their own practice sessions just before the webinar begins. You can even "promote" an attendee to be a panelist so they can ask a question, then "demote" them back to attendee. (You might want to call that last action something different.)

Above all, encourage attendees to be natural in their delivery and their interaction with each other. The less you make someone's assignment into a "Presentation" (with a capital "P"), the less pressure people will feel.

Another way to stay human: avoid choosing webinar speakers who are tech wizards but are dismal at talking to people. We've all experienced these encounters. In fact, it's an extremely common phenomenon among the big tech companies. The organizers of these events have lost sight of an essential principle, choosing to go with techie heroes rather than skilled communicators.

5

Introduce Yourself with Ease and Confidence

Want to remain calm, focused, and on top of your game when you're new to a group or meeting? Here's how to introduce yourself in the virtual setting.

"Before we get started, let's have everyone introduce themselves."

Uh-oh!

Can anything turn a poised professional into a quivering blob of jelly more quickly than a meeting where that suggestion is made? It doesn't matter if the meeting is in-person or virtual: it's a moment that's greeted with universal dread.

No wonder we can become anxious at these moments. After all, they are extreme examples of the "Introductions make me awkward" experience. If you tend toward that mindset, what could be worse than to have the moment draw visibly nearer—moment by excruciating moment—as one by one everyone on screen steps up to the firing line?

Give me a round or two with a heavyweight contender any day.

The Introductions Silver Lining

Self-introductions needn't spur nervousness and anxiety, however. For one thing, they are opportunities to get started immediately in reaching your goals for the meeting. So, for every team member, they require the same approach as other types of public speaking: a concern with meeting the audience's need rather than your own.

Again, that approach works equally well for today's video conferences as for in-person speaking.

Breathe to Calm and Focus Yourself

Whether it's waiting to be put on the spot by talking about yourself, or any other circumstance that tests your mettle, breathing is the key to self-equilibrium. It's part of knowing how to calm your nerves before speaking.

If you're like many of my speech coaching clients, you may be thinking: "Should I breathe this way throughout the meeting?" Yes, you should. Breathing fully and consciously will certainly aid your poise and the quality of your voice. But even more important, slow effortless breathing makes you better prepared for whatever is coming your way. That includes, of course, virtual conferences where you know hundreds of people will be watching.

Listen to What the Others Are Saying

Tell the truth: When you're waiting for the Dreaded Introduction to land in your lap, are you paying attention to what anyone else is saying? Of course not. You're silently rehearsing what you're going to say so you'll sound good and impress everyone.

No wonder you and everybody else are stressed out! Every presenter or discussion participant is concerned with how they're going to come across. What about the task you're all there for: to make the other people in the meeting learn something? It flies out the virtual window!

Actually listening to others' introductions, however, will help in two ways: 1) It will stop your self-consciousness and awareness of the doomsday clock you hear ticking; and 2) You will learn some things, including information you may be able to comment on or add to.

Make Your Introduction Part of Your Performance

In a virtual chat recently, I spoke with a friend I hadn't seen in a while. He confessed that he was struggling with introducing himself in online meetings. In fact, he was part of an upcoming panel at a Zoom conference, so he urgently asked my advice.

I told him about the approach I discuss in this chapter, including this point: your presentation actually begins when you introduce yourself. People will remember the impression you make now. So don't think of your self-introduction as an awkward exercise. It should be part of your game plan. Ask yourself: "What can I say at this moment that links into my message?"

For instance, let's say you're a member of your company's IT team. You're meeting with a bank's payment division to improve the process of automated financial transactions. Your company has just realized an approval step is missing, and has called the virtual meeting.

You might say something like: "I'm glad to be here because my job is xxxx. As you all know, that's an important part of our agenda today in terms of correcting this issue. So I'm looking forward to working with your staff."

If every member of your team does the same, your side has started to get your message across before any of the formal "presentations" begin!

Focus on What You Have to Contribute

Finally, remember that you're there to contribute to the overall effort and not for your personal glory. Your participation in this meeting was never about you. That may sound harsh, but it's actually the kind of positive self-talk you should practice concerning all of your public speaking. (Call it "tough love" for your own good!)

GARY GENARD

Without it, you run the risk of separating your introductory remarks from what you'll say afterwards. No wonder you feel put on the spot and at a loss. Don't worry about sounding boastful. Just make whatever you say relevant to the objective of the meeting. That's not only efficient and purposeful. It's also an easy-to-follow signpost that leads to serving the group, not yourself.

6

Presentation Skills for the Virtual Environment

Your business is online now in terms of presenting to others. Are you and your colleagues in command of the new medium? Here's how to maximize your presentation skills for the virtual environment.

Covid-19 has changed how the world conducts much of its business. In some sectors, everything is handled digitally now. And that means an explosion in the number of online meetings and conferences.

Have you and your team pivoted your presentation skills to meet this challenge?

If you (and the rest of the staff) are feeling isolated and anxious about video-based communication, paradoxically, you're not alone. Yet it still helps to know how to achieve presence and charisma, even when you're speaking online.

Here are two ways to interact with others more naturally and successfully when a webcam becomes your best friend!

Are You Coming Across the Right Way?

I recently read the following opinion, concerning how we all need to communicate online now: that doing so is "somewhere between absence and presence." This is nonsense. Why would you need to be present while online any less than you do in person? The main difference between the two situations is that one is electronically transmitted. In either case, you still need the presence that comes from authenticity. It may not be "stage" presence. Let's call it instead virtual presence.

Can you learn this type of presence? Of course. When it comes to video-based coaching and training, we have marvelous tools today in any of the online meeting platforms. Because I coach and train people from all over the world in The Genard Method of performance-based public speaking, I have been using the Pro version of Zoom since before the pandemic.

One of the nice things about video meetings (and my clients have been commenting on this), is how well it fosters in-real-time conversations when you have no other option.

So if you want to communicate strongly in video meetings, don't think of it as an "absence" that the current crisis is forcing upon you. Consider, for one thing, that most of the time you're very close to your screen—and so is everybody else.

That's actually a form of intimacy. (I won't even mention how cozy you feel wearing jammies when no one else can see it!)

Here's another way to make your presentation skills pay off online: accept how easy it is to deal with your slides while you're speaking. Instead of splitting your attention between listeners and the display screen (as many presenters do in in-person meetings), it's all now literally at your fingertips.

It should be even easier, then, to pay attention to your slides and listeners at the same time. You're already looking in the direction of both! It's one way to know how to stay focused when you're speaking. If the camera on your laptop, phone, or tablet intimidates you, see my next point.

How to Be at Your Virtual Best

I'll admit that for many people, speaking into a webcam with no one else around seems odd. For instance, it may be hard to motivate yourself for a keynote if you can't see the whole audience. This problem can be magnified if you're presenting a webinar, when you have to speak for a long time before the relief of someone "raising their hand" to ask a question.

Until recently, speaking only to a camera (that is, in a remote interview) meant that you were probably a politician, diplomat, sports commentator, or law enforcement official. Occasionally, you might have been a CEO, CFO, lawyer, medical professional, or crisis coordinator. But today, that category means all of us who are speaking to webcams on our desktops.

Let's face it: it's a challenge for any of us to relate to that unblinking eye that's activated when we hit the video button. The thought that there will be hundreds of people tuning in—or many thousands if the event is uploaded to the Internet—certainly doesn't help! So I recommend this: imagine that you're speaking, not to that webcam, but to someone whose opinion you value greatly.

This person may be a colleague, spouse, sibling, mentor, or your wise uncle. It should be a person you really would like to hear say, "Denise [or Dan or Deja] . . . that was terrific! You really hit it out of the park." When you imagine you're talking to that person when you present (instead of a digital device), you come across at your best—as you would in a natural conversation with someone whose opinion is worth hearing.

All good public speaking is conversational. It doesn't matter if it takes place in a boardroom, convention hall, or over the phone. Or these days, via a video conference.

7

Great Presentations Need Powerful Openings

Presenting with impact and influence means starting out strongly. Here's how you and your team can create a powerful opening each time you present.

These days, you and the rest of your staff are dealing with meeting after meeting on virtual platforms. But despite the sheer number of meet-ups, there's still a moment of drama before each presentation begins. Although cyberspace may make that interval a bit shorter than in a live meeting, it's still there. And if you're the one presenting, you need to use it to your advantage.

It's all about anticipation. Of course, people are also thinking at this moment: "I hope this holds my attention and has something I can use."

You Have a Captive Audience. There's no doubt that your virtual audience is paying maximum attention at the kick-off moment. They are primed for whatever they're about to experience. Sometimes they will have no idea of your speaking ability. And the more meetings they're sitting in on, the more they will be hoping that yours is the one contribution that's going to be interesting and engaging.

The first sixty seconds are especially important, since that's the time that judgments and decisions are made about you and your topic. Here are four strategies that you should always follow as you open your talk. If you want listeners to feel they're in good company, do these four things, in the following order.

1) Grab 'Em at the Start

Consider how most presenters begin: "Hi, everybody. Today I'll be talking about . . ." This is typically followed by slides, some of them with way too much information on them. If you're not hearing anybody groaning, it's probably because they're too polite. (Or maybe they just muted their audio!)

This initial moment is such valuable real estate that it's shocking presenters don't spend any time making it interesting. Let's face it: to be good as a speaker, you have to know how to start a speech.

There are rhetorical devices, however, that have been successful for centuries in getting listeners interested immediately. Here are a dozen of them that you and your fellow team members can use:

- Story

- Question

- Statistic

- Startling statement

- Personal anecdote

- Humor (not a joke!)

- Demonstration

- Expert opinion

- Hot topic in the industry

- Case study

- "Imagine . . ."

- Today's headline or top online story

You don't have the luxury of taking a few minutes to find your groove. You must show everyone right away that you're going to be interesting so they start listening. Once that happens, it's much easier to keep them there.

2) Make Your Topic Sound Interesting

At this point, without going any further into your remarks, tell everyone specifically what you're going to be talking about.

Even if participants know your topic ahead of time, you lose nothing by reminding them about it here. Besides, this is your opportunity to pique their interest. Let's say you're giving a talk as part of your town library's online lecture series. You could start off by saying, "My topic today is migrating birds of the Northeast." Or you could offer this instead: "Today, you'll be meeting some of the most eccentric characters you could ever run into . . . who just happen to be sitting outside your window right now."

Which talk sounds more interesting?

3) Tell Them Why They Need to Listen

Here is the most neglected family member of tasks you should accomplish in your opening. It's the moment you tell everyone what your topic has to do with them.

This is a huge part of engaging virtual participants and getting them to pay close attention. And as I say, many presenters never even give it a thought. But consider this: every member of every webcast is in a "What's-in-it-for-me?" frame of mind when they join a meeting. They're wondering if this is going to be worth their time.

If you answer their question in a way that relates to their job or interest and makes the payoff clear, they will tune in. "I want to discuss this today because it's going to make your life much easier," is a great way to begin. So be specific in terms of the benefit to the participants. Believe me, their ears will perk up.

4) Give Them a Roadmap of Your Journey Together

So, let's review. You've 1) grabbed your audience's attention, 2) made your topic sound interesting, and 3) told them why it's worthwhile for them to listen. You're ready for the final part of your opening: giving them a roadmap of where you'll be going together.

Call it a blueprint if you like that metaphor. (I prefer roadmap because it presupposes that there will be signposts along the way.) Partly, this helps make your subject manageable. Whatever the topic, it's too big to talk about in its entirety. So you have to clue listeners in to the sub-topic areas you'll be addressing in this meeting. It may sound something like this:

"I'll be talking about three specific elements of [reaching this goal, gaining this proficiency, understanding what you're looking at, etc.]. First, we'll examine [your first main point]. Once we have that information, we'll be able to [discuss your second item]. At that point, we'll be able to look at [your last main point]."

As the great salesman Dale Carnegie once advised: "Tell the audience what you're going to say, say it; then tell them what you've said." In other words, invite them on an interesting journey; take them there; then remind them of what an enlightening virtual trip it's been.

8

Getting to the Point and Speaking Concisely

Do you take online meeting participants round and round the mulberry bush? Here's how to get to the point and speak concisely.

In Shakespeare's *Hamlet,* the character Polonius informs King Claudius and Queen Gertrude that, "brevity is the soul of wit." This wise remark is nevertheless hilarious, since Polonius is a notorious windbag. In fact, it takes him six lines to get to the point. (I once played the part, but I sincerely hope you don't believe in typecasting.)

To avoid making brevity a custom more honored in the breach than the observance (also *Hamlet*), let's discuss conciseness. Why should we? Because it's necessary for leadership and shows you have a sharp mind. It's also a good practice for online meetings where many people need to be heard.

Your Mission as a Presenter

Why don't people speak concisely, anyway? (I know that you do!) It isn't because they were born under a wandering star. It's just that, with SO MUCH INFORMATION available, they want to get it all in. That's usually a guarantee of a muddled message.

Here's a true story from my practice that illustrates this. A few months ago, a director in a large corporation sent one of her managers to me. Her department at the parent company oversaw eight subsidiaries.

Naturally, there was a history of friction in this relationship. There were many reasons for this, but much of it boiled down to a feeling on the part of the smaller companies that the message was always: "We're the big guys. So just shut up and do what we say."

The manager and her boss at the parent company were frustrated. It seemed that every time the manager led an online meeting of the subsidiary leadership teams, the results were unproductive and she herself was unhappy.

In my work with her, I discovered the reason: each time, the manager tried to bring too many injuries from old battles into the meeting. Believing that she would end up defending her every position, she would get ready to address any complaint the subsidiary leadership might bring up about anything in the past.

Preparing in that way, I told her, predisposed her to go down side paths, pulling her off the main road. Among other things, it meant that already tiring virtual meetings came to seem like an endless waste of time.

I used this analogy in my discussion with her: it was as if she entered a room that contained a four-foot fish tank, pulling behind her a beluga whale! Meetings—virtual or not—are small windows of opportunity that close fast. Each participant needs to be self-disciplined enough to stay on point. That's especially true of the host. And part of staying on point is getting to the point.

They Corral Horses, Don't They?

Here's another visualization that will help you and your team accomplish your task. Think of the information you need to get across in terms of a corral—or what we call in the Eastern U.S., a paddock.

What's a corral or paddock for? To keep horses confined so they can't wander all over the place, right? Your visualized "verbal corral" can help accomplish the same task when it comes to keeping your remarks within limits.

It involves a two-step process: First, frame your topic the same way a corral creates a defined space for those horses. Rather than making a remark without knowing exactly where your narrative will lead from there, make it a little harder on yourself. Be clear on what you're going to talk about, so you have to stick with that and no more.

E.g., "Today, I'm going to discuss getting our products more efficiently from Quality Control to the loading docks." That doesn't leave you much room to digress about, say, drivers' complaints. And that's a good thing.

Second, build your corral. In our example, that may sound like this: "There are three important steps we need to follow: (1) Labeling the boxes after the products are inspected; (2) Forklift and conveyer belt operations; and (3) Completing the shipping manifests at the docks." Now it's easy for you to stay focused and on point because you've given yourself no other options!

Feel free to run around (a little) within the corral you've built. Just don't get any ideas about jumping over any of the gates.

9

How to Keep Everyone Engaged

Here's an actor's tool to help you make things easy for virtual audiences. It involves the best way to keep participants engaged.

When it comes to influencing online audiences, you'd better know how to engage listeners at all times.

So, let's talk about how to keep participants tuned in throughout your presentation. This is also about how to make things easy for them in terms of retaining key information.

It involves a dramatic concept known as "beats." It's an essential part of The Genard Method of achieving presence and charisma as a speaker. And it applies equally whether you're delivering your remarks in person or online. (For virtual meetings, the technique is also a powerful tool when each of your team members practices it.)

An Actor's Technique for Public Speaking

What a "beat" is: A beat in a play or movie concerns a character's intention in a scene. Think of it as the motivation driving that character's actions. The stronger that motivation is, the more the actor has to "play."

A character in a script is activated by that motivation until one of two things happens. Either a) he or she accomplishes their objective, or b) they fail to do so, for any reason. Whichever happens, that beat gives way to a new one. It's one of the ways actors understand what makes a character tick, and why they take the action they do in the script.

For instance, Dianna Demure (a character in a movie I just made up) is a teller who is embezzling money from the bank. Right now, in fact, she has a stack of bills inside an envelope in her purse. In this scene of her getting ready to leave for the day, her intention (her "beat") is to keep bank president I.M. Rich from knowing the truth.

But as she's reaching for her coat, her purse tips sideways and the envelope falls to the floor, spilling out $100 bills. Mr. Rich happens to be walking by, sees what just happened, and says, "Ms. Demure . . . what's that?"

At this point, Dianna's intention to hide her theft ends (since that motivation is now useless). A new intention or beat must begin. Depending on the script, that might be to talk her way out of the situation, to feign ignorance of the envelope, to confess and throw herself on Mr. Rich's mercy, etc.

How this relates to public speaking: An acting beat like the one we just witnessed is comparable to each *main point* in your presentation (or that of each member of your team). When you speak, you naturally concern yourself with discussing each main point with listeners, before you go on to the next item in your agenda.

Let's say you plan to discuss three important items within your topic. Like the actor, you must make it clear at different points that you have finished with this item, and are about to start discussing the next one.

This is important because it allows listeners to pay maximum attention to each area you're discussing (or "beat"). If you don't make it obvious where the transitions are, your talk can begin to seem too long, with too much data accumulating. Combined with the screen fatigue that can come from too many Zoom calls, this can seriously crimp your ability to keep people tuned in.

For participants to keep paying attention, that is, you have to give them information in bite-sized pieces. You offer one hearty bite per segment, as it were, and allow them to "chew" and "digest" that point before you offer them another bite (the food metaphor works well here). Each segment of your talk is a "beat," since what you intend to get across is unique to that point.

Listeners can then absorb the information you're giving them and be ready for the next bite. (Alternately, here's another metaphor: you allow them to hit the "refresh" button in their mind each time you go on to a different sub-topic.) Whichever way you think about it, you're helping listeners keep pace with you and the data you're presenting, while boosting everyone's ability to retain key points.

How to "Play Your Beats"

Obviously, you're not acting in your virtual meetings. How, then, do you use this technique as a presenter who knows how to captivate her or his audience? It's really very easy. You only have to do two things as your "beat" changes. Here's all it involves:

1. Pause. The more major the change between segments, the longer the pause should be. For instance, the transitions between the intro and the body, and the body and the conclusion, are bigger than the ones between each main point within the body. For those transitions, your pauses can be shorter.

2. Do something different with your voice. That's intentionally vague. It really doesn't matter what you do, because it's the change that perks up everyone's ears.

You can go up in pitch, or down in pitch. You can change the quality of your voice. You might alter the pace at which you're speaking; or you could even ask a rhetorical question, e.g., "What should our company do to solve this problem?"

Those two changes in your delivery—a significant pause, and a difference in your voice—are enough to alert participants that you're moving on to the next segment of your talk. Everyone can exhale, refresh themselves mentally, and be ready to absorb your next point.

10

What Your Company Needs to Know to Stay Ahead of the Competition

How is your business adapting to the digital world? Here's why online public speaking training is more important than ever.

Online public speaking coaching and training has been an important source of communication skills improvement for a long time. But there's never been such a need for it as there is now.

Once a convenience, virtual speaking is now at the core of how you and your staff communicate. Screen-based learning and practice no longer approximate business dealings—they're now the real thing. The better your team or department gets at it, the more persuasive and influential they will be in the digital world.

There's also this thought: in a shrinking business universe, you need to know how to pitch yourself or your company better than the competition. Period.

Online Public Speaking Courses Work!

If you personally have had speech coaching or provided corporate public speaking training for your employees, then you know the value of in-person sessions or workshops. But we're in a different world now. Corporate travel and in-person meetings are now discouraged or prohibited outright. We heard early in the current crisis about conferences that sent

Covid-19-positive attendees dispersing worldwide—one of them right here in the city where my company is based, Boston.

Even before the current crisis, we were living in an increasingly visual world. One of the best aspects of video-based training is that it's strongly visual. There's not only the face-to-face intimacy allowed by webcams. Your coach or trainer can also include slides or any other visual element he or she would use in an in-person workshop or private session. And every virtual platform now allows screen recording for critiques and feedback.

Combining Online and On-Site Training

And here's a heads-up for that big event your company is planning (whenever you're able to go forward with it). Virtual coaching beforehand of your speaker line-up can be combined with an on-site rehearsal the day of your event. I've conducted a number of these hybrid trainings that are ideal for organizations with widespread personnel.

Even though such events are off the table for now, you can still help your employees improve by keeping the online portions of the training going. There's even an argument for going forward with such training now, so your speakers are in the best possible shape when the event draws near, and they have a hundred other things on their minds. (By the same reasoning, now may be the time to work on an online option for getting over your fear of public speaking.)

And of course, online training makes perfect sense when your staff is actually presenting virtually. That's certainly the case now.

You may be limited to working from home these days. But you have one of the most powerful resources—online public speaking training—literally at your fingertips. It's a great tool for making you and your team more polished and effective speakers, without the headaches of travel budgets and scheduling. You can bet that right now your competition is absolutely considering it.

11

Do Your Team Members Speak Like This? — It Hurts Their Credibility!

Does one's vocal style matter in terms of influencing listeners? You'd better believe it! For instance, if your team members speak like this, it can hurt their credibility.

Is your voice helping or hurting your career? How about the others on your team as well as your company's profile—what's the reputation the firm is developing in your industry? Are customers and prospects turning off because of how you pitch your products, services, or ideas in terms of speaking styles?

These may not be questions you've ever asked yourself. But believe me, they can make a difference to individual and organizational success. So they're definitely questions worth considering.[4]

Recently, for instance, I was hired by a federal government agency to coach one of their key employees. This person is a high-ranking and valued member of the team. But the individual's speaking style was making potential vendors uneasy in online meetings. In the context of these meetings—where one's speaking ability is that much more in the spotlight—it was an area this agency knew it had to address.

A speaker's vocal style affects everything from their credibility and authority, to their persuasiveness and likability. (The

---

[4] In this chapter, I'll discuss vocal skills in terms of individual contributions. I believe that will help make these suggestions personal in nature. If your group presents ideas through group chanting, however, then by all means think collectively!

same goes, of course, concerning the organization they're representing.) Given the importance of the voice to human interactions, this shouldn't be a surprise. I suspect that lately, the constant need to interact intimately in virtual situations has brought voice and speech issues even more into the spotlight.

Two aspects of your speech performance in particular can limit you professionally. Let's talk about each of them.

Don't Talk Faster than a Speeding Bullet

Superman may be faster than a speeding bullet (and in the old TV intro to each episode, able to leap tall buildings in a single bound). But the rest of us need to keep our listeners in mind and not fly by them at supersonic speeds.

If rapid speech is an issue for you, you may already have received feedback about it. If not, start noticing if meeting participants lean forward toward their screen or wear a slight frown when you speak. They may simply be trying to understand what you're saying. That can be a challenge for them if words and thoughts come at them faster than they're able to absorb or feel comfortable with.

This can also be a problem in phone conversations or conference calls, where all visual clues are removed. Yet if it's a habit with you, it most likely will be present whenever you speak, including when you're not excited about anything. One of the reasons this can be such a disadvantage, is that fast speakers may not even be aware that people are uncomfortable listening to them.

If you're a speed-speaker, record yourself to build your awareness (and to hear yourself starting to slow down). Even more fundamental is breathing properly, i.e., making sure you take enough breaths. Mother Nature has arranged things so that we can't inhale and speak at the same time. I get the feeling she knew what she was doing.

I'm Serious: You Need Gravitas as a Speaker!

grav•i•tas noun 1. dignity, seriousness, or solemnity of manner.[5]

A lack of gravitas or authority in your speech is the second weakness that can seriously affect your credibility. And believe me, I'm serious when I say you need seriousness as a speaker!

Dickens's character Scrooge may have thought that there was "more of gravy than of grave" in the ghost of his partner Marley (that is, his appearance was due simply to a bit of indigestion on Scrooge's part). But

---

[5] https://www.google.com/search?q=gravitas&rlz=1C5ACMJ_enU-S521US521&oq=gravitas&aqs=chrome.0.69i59j0l6j69i60.1743j0j7&sourcei-d=chrome&ie=UTF-8

gravitas in terms of maturity and experience can announce itself through your speaking style.

Wikipedia offers this marvelous take on the word:

Gravitas was one of the ancient Roman virtues that denoted "seriousness". It is also translated variously as weight, dignity, and importance and connotes restraint and moral rigor. It also conveys a sense of responsibility and commitment to the task.[6]

Obviously, then, sounding like you are experienced plays an important part in persuading stakeholders that you're credible and authoritative. To cite one example from my practice: a company hired me to work with a group of talented young salespeople who, unfortunately, sounded that way. The

---

[6] https://en.wikipedia.org/wiki/Gravitas

company discovered that it was tough for prospective customers to decide to spend big with a sales staff who (in the prospects' minds) sounded like kids.

Could that have been an unfair judgment? Sure. But if you sense that customers and clients may be viewing you or your team that way, work on that gravitas!

12

How to Be a Star in Your Next Video Conference

Want to shine bright in Zoom meetings? Here's how to be a star in your next video conference.

Whatever else the current crisis has brought about, it's given us a new window on virtual communications. In one sense that's literally true. The world of business is being transformed through the "windows" of our computers, tablets, and phone screens.

We've learned—and continue to learn—much from digital meetings. In fact, we could probably all write a book together titled How to Succeed in Business Using Zoom.

It's clear, then, that you've been cast in a new drama debuting on the world's screens. How can you become a star in this new role? Here are five ways to nail the kind of performance you'll be proud of when the webcam starts rolling.

1. Be in Position When the Camera Rolls

Can you imagine anything more embarrassing than an actor scurrying into place on the set when the camera is already on? Yet every day, video-meeting attendees—professionals all—can be seen performing the Zoom Scramble.

When you join a virtual meeting, you should be in position ready to make an impression. The truth is, you're already doing so. The other attendees shouldn't see you carting your laptop into the room, or searching everywhere on the screen for the right buttons. By now, you should know how to get the connection working, so it's seamless and already taken care of when you join the meeting.

And please, get the height of your laptop right! Too many Zoomers are living in Brobdingnag,* peering down on the world while everyone looks up their nostrils.

2. Know Your Intentions in the Scene

Contributing in video meetings is exactly like acting in one respect: the truth the persona you're showing us is more important than your lines. (Indeed, in "theater of the absurd" plays, the lines seem, well, absurd, and meaning must be found elsewhere.)

In the online meeting world, it's easy to turn on the firehouse of data, and many people do. But we should always ask ourselves, even before we put together our content: "What's my purpose in speaking to these listeners?" Once you're clear on what you're trying to get across, your intentions and the way you present your story will be in synch. Just like an actor with a character.

3. Stay in Character

Speaking of character—don't "drop" yours. What the other people in a webcast see is your presentation persona. It's no different from what takes place when you present in person. That means, for one thing, that you can't slip into the at-home environment so much that your professionalism suffers. (Think twice, for instance, before getting up to fetch that glass of water if you're wearing exercise shorts.)

It also means having the discipline to stay focused. Always keep in mind what others are seeing. Video meetings have more in common with the theater than they do with movies, for instance. When you watch a play, your gaze isn't captive—you can look at whatever is happening onstage. Films, on the other hand, force you to look only where the camera directs your gaze.

So a video meeting is a bit like a play: just because someone is speaking doesn't mean that we have to look at him or her. We can "peek" in on others, or change our screen mode in terms of whom we're seeing (this is especially the case for the host).

It can be exhausting to stay in your professional persona, call after call. But you need to do it. And hey, it's better than sitting in traffic or on a runway, right?

4. Be Ready to Move Meeting Members

By all means, establish your credibility with your deep knowledge of the topic. But don't forget about emotion.

This is usually more important in internal video conferences than those with a customer or other external audiences. But many of us are constantly in departmental or intra-company online meetings. And in those, showing empathy for team members or colleagues is paramount.

Even with clients, there will be times when you want to demonstrate your commitment or passion for an idea or solution. If you don't sound emotionally committed, why should anyone believe that you have skin in the game?

It's been said that an actor can break your heart at fifty feet. Nowadays, it may be necessary for you to move listeners at a distance of 2,000 or 7,000 miles.

5. Use Your Performance Skills, Including Emotion

It's easy to consider video conferences as substitutes for "real" in-person interactions. You might, for instance, think that you can't speak dynamically when you're stuck in front of a small screen.

Yet your job is still to use your performance skills to make the material come to life. Data void of context and humanity is as dull when delivered on a screen as it is in person.

Actors don't diminish the passion they feel as the character (though they may display it differently) because they know the show will be on TV rather than on stage!

If you think it's boring to watch someone sitting stiffly in front of a webcam reading from slides or notes—you're right. Therefore, you can't do that. Although great in terms of actual distance, your video presence is digitally just two feet away.

That's the distance of intimacy. (Just don't lean in when you get excited and make the connection too intimate!)

Invest yourself fully in what you're saying. Use vocal coloration, facial expressions, and focused eye contact. Go ahead and gesture. When you give it your all, everyone hears and sees your passion and commitment. If nothing else, that may help keep them awake in this seventh video of their workday.

*A fictional land in Jonathan Swift's novel, *Gulliver's Travels*, where giants lived.

13

Speaking with Warmth and Personality to a Webcam

Video conferencing has become a way of life for many of us. Here's how to share the warmth of your personality when you're in front of a webcam.

Recently, I was lucky enough to get a close-up look at Cisco's TelePresence Systems hardware options at one of the company's facilities. It was a breathtaking array of state-of-the-art video conferencing technology.

Whether you use this company's products or those of its competitors, you know by now that virtual communication is changing the face of business. Fast.

If you work for a large company or organization, you've probably known this for some time. The rest of the business world now gets it as well: virtual presence is the mode we'll be operating in more and more. A global pandemic will get that message across in no uncertain terms. But so will cost incentives, sheer efficiency, and the ability to share knowledge instantly. Therefore, the question you need to answer now is: Are you ready to communicate with your best screen persona?

Here are four ways to give a strong performance in the Theater of Virtual Presence, where the curtain has already risen.

1. Speak Directly to the Camera (It's Your Audience)

The audience watching and listening to you in a video conference is a captive one. And that, as they say, is a good thing. They can only be in one place, and it's your job to direct their gaze to the one place you're in.

In the last chapter, I introduced an analogy of theater vs. film that explains this well. When you watch a play as it's performed, you can look wherever you like to observe what's going on. You can tune into the actor who's speaking, or the other actors as they react. But you can also examine the scenery, the stage lights, or the interior of the theater itself. When you watch a film, however, your gaze is predetermined, since you can only look where the camera tells you to look.

So, while you can look anywhere you want, if you're speaking you know that everyone will be looking at you. If you want to influence the other participants while speaking, you have to look at the camera and not at, say, all the thumbnails on your screen.

This can take some getting used to. It happened with one of my clients recently. We were located in different rooms as he practiced his virtual presentation. But he never seemed to look at me once—for some reason, he kept looking off to the side.

When we watched the recording, it was immediately obvious that he was looking at me—but the real me in the room, not the virtual one, i.e., the camera. (I was sitting in a corner of the room away from the monitor while videotaping the session.) If this had been an actual meeting, he would appear not to have been speaking to his listeners at all. In this case, it was an easy fix to get him to direct his gaze at the camera.

Teach yourself that the camera IS your audience. Once you get your gaze right, you'll come through as warm and genuine, and talking directly to everyone. In our second taping in my client session, the difference was positive and dramatic.

2. Hands Away From Face!

As you will know if you've ever been interviewed on a talk show, or even sat too close to the lens while videotaping: cameras magnify everything. Something as innocent as flicking your gaze to the side in a live shot will make you look shifty.

Therefore, keep that gaze steady and true. A special precaution: If you're too dependent on your notes or your computer screen, you'll be looking away from the viewer too often, and you'll make no emotional connection.

Another innocent habit that can work against you in a virtual setting is touching your face. Again, the static nature of the camera's eye makes anything that takes place in its limited visual field noticeable.

Hands to the face looks fidgety and is likely to pull people's attention away from what you're saying. Think of it as one of those things you do when you're alone (as you may seem to be when speaking virtually) that you wouldn't want others to see.

3. Body Language Applies to Your Top Half Too

Well, if the above is true concerning touching your face, what should you do with your hands? Since you may feel like you're glued to a chair with the webcam's eye scrutinizing your every move, won't moving your hands at all be distracting?

Actually, it won't. Body language doesn't only apply to your bottom half after all. Using natural, strong gestures to support what you're saying is just as important if you're sitting down. In fact, people in online meetings who sit stiffly and seem afraid to move are uncomfortable to watch.

Feel free to gesture naturally. Just be sure the size of the gesture is appropriate, i.e., try to keep it within the width of your body so your hands and arms aren't flailing outward. Gestures made the right way look well defined and controlled. They give the impression that you're in control.

4. Personalizing a Microphone or Camera

Finally, perhaps the most challenging aspect of speaking virtually is personalizing the mic and webcam. You are at your best when you speak to people, not to a recording instrument. The whole idea of a teleconference, after all, is that you reach people with your presence, rather than just throwing data at everyone.

But speaking virtually means, of course, that you can't be physically present for everyone. During the times when you are literally all alone—e.g., being interviewed remotely for a news program, participating in a video conference, or speaking by phone during a radio show—you have no one to speak to except that microphone and camera.

So how do you project the essence of your personality to a cold recording instrument? You can't. Instead, you have to make it human. As I mentioned earlier in Chapter 6 on presentation skills, imagine that the camera or mic is someone whose opinion you care deeply about. It can be a colleague, spouse, child, best friend, mentor, or anyone else. Make it someone you know well, whom you want to say at the end of your remarks, "That was really good. That's the you I admire. I'm proud of you."

You'll be amazed at how the "genuine you" comes through loud and clear. Provided you're using a good virtual meeting product to make the connection, you'll have the best of all possible teleworlds.

14

Vocal Skills for the Virtual Environment

Do your vocal skills help you move listeners and accomplish your business goals? Here's how to improve your voice for the virtual environment.

Let's consider one of your most attractive qualities for succeeding virtually in business.

I'm talking about your voice.

Does that surprise you?

Didn't you ever listen to someone, male

or female, and have one of two thoughts: a) "I can't stand this person's voice!" or b) "I could listen to this person talk all day long"?

Our reaction to the way people sound is partly primal and unconscious. Some of that has to do with survival, of course. But the human voice is also unsurpassed when it comes to giving us clues about a person's personality and intentions. Then there are all the subtler aspects of spoken communication, such as reasonableness, warmth, power, confidence, persuasiveness, and many other qualities. All of these factors play out even more strongly in the absence of full-body nonverbal clues that are absent in virtual encounters.

In fact, your voice is the most valuable performance tool you own for public speaking. Yet unless some particular vocal issue bothers you, you probably don't think about it much. I'd like to remedy that situation—at least for the time it takes you to read this chapter.

Creating a Powerful and Authoritative Voice

Listeners make judgments about you quickly—and your voice announces some things about you right away. Unfortunately, the characteristics you're advertising may not reflect who you are at all. That's usually because you've never been trained in the productive use of the voice. (Don't feel lonely, however. Our education systems and even business training rarely include much on effective oral communication.)

For instance, a thin "head voice" can make you sound young and lacking in experience. A too-soft voice seems to reveal a lack of assertiveness, and so on.

Conversely, power and authority broadcast themselves through a strong, resonant voice. In fact, when we speak about "the sound of leadership," vocal attributes are literally part of the equation. As a leader, your voice needs to carry, be well supported (i.e., keep the sound of the words buoyant without trailing away), and reflect maturity and experience.

For your voice to reflect true power, however, it also has to sound quietly confident. You won't assert your authority in a positive way by simply shouting out your ideas louder than anyone else. The way to create a pleasant, resonant, and confident voice is through the right method of breathing. That means using your diaphragm to create a full reservoir of air to support and project your sound, while providing a "cushion" so your voice is pleasant rather than strident.

Incidentally, this is all the more important when you're sitting for long periods in virtual meetings. Even a slight relaxation in your posture means compressing the breathing mechanism so that your capacity for a full breath is diminished.

Breathing for Speaking

Controlled breathing is essential, then, for increasing your power and authority while keeping your voice attractive.

The idea behind breathing diaphragmatically for speaking is twofold: first, to get a sufficient volume of air in your lungs; and second, to project that air outwards strongly enough so that your voice sounds full and carries well. You can feel when you're accomplishing the second part of that equation in your belly area.

Place your hand on your abdomen, just above the belly button. Your belly should move inward when you exhale. That contraction of the diaphragm creates a column of air that moves up your throat toward the voice box. There, your vocal folds respond by vibrating, producing the voice. (You can really feel this inward movement of the abdomen by keeping your hand on your belly and saying, "Hey!" loudly.)

Simple physics tells us that more force, i.e., a stronger column of air moving upwards, will result in more vibration of the vocal folds—like wind chimes acted upon by a strong breeze. The result is more powerful sound waves, which translates into a stronger voice.

If you can do this while keeping your throat open rather than tight and straining (which is what happens when you shout), the result is a voice that achieves power while staying attractive to the ear. That of course is the combination you need for the virtual environment, where you don't have to project the sound outward very far. Instead, you'll create the impression of quiet confidence that I mentioned earlier.

15

How to Make What You Say Sound Important

Can you get others in an online meeting to pay attention when you have a great idea? Here's how to make what you say sound important.

In the last chapter, I discussed how you can improve your voice for the virtual environment. I mentioned, first, the importance of the voice; and second, ways that you can produce a well-supported, pleasant, and authoritative sound.

Now I'd like to build on that information, by discussing how you can speak with more emphasis and energy regarding key words and phrases. Doing so is critical to making what you say sound important.

How to Get Your Ideas Across Effectively

Can a speaker have a great idea that is nevertheless expressed badly? Certainly. One principal reason can be lack of energy in vocal delivery. Most of the time, that's caused by poor breath support. Here's why.

As you now know, speech results from an exhaled column of air that is acted upon by the vocal folds in the larynx. When these membranes vibrate, they create a pulse of air, which is amplified by resonators in the body.[7] It's the air, then (from your

---

[7] https://voicefoundation.org/health-science/voice-disorders/anatomy-physi-ology-of-voice-production/understanding-voice-production/

exhalation) that allows your voice to carry well enough to be heard by others.

In other words, you need enough air to "support" the sound all the way through to the end of the idea. Now, in spoken English, the most important word or phrase usually comes at the end of a thought, not the beginning or middle. ("We want to be recognized, not just as a player, but as *the leader in our industry.*")

If your voice trails off because you don't have enough air, listeners will either a) not hear the right emphasis that makes the meaning clear, or b) miss what you said completely. In either case, lack of energy robs listeners of something they need to know. And that puts a serious crimp in your effectiveness in online meetings.

To Convey Importance, That Is the Question!

The solution is obvious. To make what you say sound important, you need to punch key words and phrases—to make them peaks in the vocal landscape—so they become prominent. Consider this: though you know which words those are in the context of your talk, your audience won't until you let them hear it!

Tape yourself and listen to whether you trail off at the ends of sentences, or give the thought enough vocal support until the end. If you do the latter, listeners will both hear and grasp the significance of what you're saying.

Remember, Hamlet said, "To be or not to be, that is the QUESTION." If he'd said instead, "The question is whether to be or not," you'd probably be asking yourself now: "What's a Hamlet?"

16

Body Language: How to Look Great on Video

Concerned with your appearance and presence in online meetings? Here are some essential body language tips on how to look great on video.

We all know how important body language is when it comes to sensing people's attitudes, intentions, and feelings. Not surprisingly, research in this area has focused on in-person and not virtual interactions. And it has mostly concerned what someone is showing as they respond to you.

But for years now, I've been writing about the other side: what you do as a speaker that gives audiences clues about who you are.

Now that online meetings are so important, a reset is in order. We need to know what works in the video world. Body language, like video itself, is a visual element. It has tremendous power to shape others' opinions of your honesty, credibility, and trustworthiness (among many other qualities).

That means you're as dependent upon it in online engagements as in-person. It means, in fact, that you must use the language of the body when speaking virtually. The fact that you are limited to a small screen is irrelevant—nonverbal communication is still hugely important to your success. Below are three ways you can use body language well in any and all video appearances.

Face It: Facial Expressions Are a Picture of Your Mind

Start with the most important virtual body language tool—the face. Your face takes precedence over full-body language online for the simple reason that it's mostly what meeting participants see. There is simply too much of your body that's excluded in a video call for it to be your primary tool of nonverbal expression. Because your face now fills the screen, it has taken over the starring role.

There are forty-three muscles in the face . . . and they are all there for a reason. The Roman statesman Cicero said: "The face is a picture of the mind with the eyes as its interpreter." Online where your face fills the screen, that "picture" is a vital part of how others experience and understand you. Importantly, it's also part of how they perceive you and judge your intentions.

For instance, we "leak" emotions through our facial expressions, even when we don't intend for it to happen. It stands to reason, therefore, that the more you're in control of what your face is revealing, the more you'll be showing what you want to be seen. (Of course, being honest in what you're saying is the most important impetus for making this happen!)

So, is your face expressive? It's a trait you should know about yourself by now. And here's something else worth knowing: facial expressions proceed from emotions, but it also works the other way around.

For instance, you know that when you're happy, you smile; and when you're sad, you look that way. But the reverse occurs as well, because your mind and body recognize how emotions and their physical manifestations are closely linked. This means that by assuming a particular facial expression, you can elicit the emotional response associated with it in both you and your listeners. Get a mirror and practice. — Use the essential body language of the face!

Nice Hands and Arms You've Got There. — Use 'Em!

Does the dominance of your face in online meetings mean that the rest of your body isn't of any use to you? Of course not. Aside from head movements and posture— body language that almost no one talks about in terms of physical expressiveness— you still own plenty of real estate that's worth showing. The whole top half of your body, in fact! (Come to think of it, even your shoulders can be expressive.)

Pay attention to fellow participants in your next few virtual meetings. You'll see that some of them use gestures quite naturally on the screen. After all, gestures exist to strengthen and amplify your statements, as well as to support or clarify what you're saying. They are a natural part of your expressiveness, and should emerge organically. When you feel strongly about something, you show it. Why would you leave out that response just because you're speaking virtually?

In fact, holding back on that impulse is a danger in video meetings. We think, "I can't really gesture here because I'm stuck in front of this small screen. It will look weird." The truth is that it will look natural . . . sitting stiffly and not moving is what looks strange!

Provided you're far enough from the screen (around 18-24"), we'll be able to see your gestures and respond to them. Just keep your hand and arm movements within an imaginary square drawn around your upper torso. That way, your "visual energy" will be centered and focused rather than dissipated.

Lean In . . . But Also Lean Out

Your distance from the screen also

comes into play in terms of displaying natural, conversational body language. That's the third of my suggestions for using nonverbal communication well on the small screen.

Statues are not only in disfavor in many of our cities these days—they also shouldn't occupy your seat in front of the video screen. So-called body language "experts" will tell you about the importance of good posture in video conferences, and fair enough. But don't eliminate movement. The human eye responds favorably to change, not sameness. If you're the one who moves naturally in virtual meetings while others sit statue-like, you'll gain ground in terms of engagement and memorability (and, I'd think, reputation).

Back to the distance from the screen: make it enough so that you can change your posture from time to time. You don't sit stone-still through an entire in-person meeting, do you? The problem with too many of today's online speakers is that they sit too close to the monitor. They're "leaning in," all right. But the person who allows more of him or her to be seen, and who leans back from time to time, is in my mind the more interesting one to watch.

Doing so looks like part of a conversation. And conversations are what all good speaking is about.

17

Do This to Become More Personable and Likable

Are you a charismatic speaker in video conferences? Here's the secret of being more personable in virtual meetings.

Do you find it easy to be committed and enthusiastic to a camera?

Many of us don't. But in the Age of Covid-19, we're being called upon to try to accomplish that trick day in and day out. We're pitching ideas, giving important updates, speaking to senior leadership, and demonstrating our knowledge and professionalism in a myriad of other ways.

And we get to stare at an unblinking camera—that we can't even see! —while doing it.

If you're at a loss as to how to accomplish this feat while embodying charisma, I have a solution for you.

Bringing Your Real Self to Your Virtual Presence

In public speaking—as in acting—what you think and feel doesn't matter much unless you can convey it to the audience. The people watching and listening to you in virtual settings are no different. They need to see and hear what's inside you if you're going to bring your true presence to the encounter.

There's a fundamental error presenters often make, however, that prevents that from happening. That's the mistake of thinking that it's the information they convey that accomplishes their purpose in the meeting.

You can see why it's easy to go down this path. Delivering essential data; conveying a complex idea; or leading participants through a bar graph all seem to be at the heart of what these speakers are trying to achieve. But those things aren't the essence of the online interaction. If they were, why would anybody need this video conference at all? Wouldn't a simple email with attachment suffice?

Why Your Performance Matters

But it doesn't, and here's why: your ability to interpret and speak to the significance of the topic is what matters. In fact, it's what makes your participation in this meeting invaluable.

Finding a way to connect with the people you're talking to, then, rather than just giving them some content, is at the heart of what you're really trying to do. In a way, your remarks should be about them as much as they are about the data you're discussing.

Let me give an example. I recently coached a client on virtually delivering an overview of her firm—a nonprofit concerned with environmental issues. The first minute or so of her remarks addressed the problems all of us are facing. Then it was time for her to say, "Won't you join with us in finding solutions?"

For this short speech to work, the tone had to change at precisely that point. The online attendees would have to feel that she was pivoting from the problem, to the need to join hands in working toward the solution.

It was a human-to-human moment, and it wasn't happening in our practice session. What she said at that moment— the heart of her pitch—sounded exactly like the previous recital of the problems.

So, for the rest of our session, I worked to get her to look directly into the camera and, basically, share her humanity.

Yes, it's hard to make a cold, unfeeling webcam into something you can relate to. But it's a key skill of speaking virtually. And it's possible if you remind yourself that it's the people, much more than the information, that matters.

My advice is to practice, practice, and practice this skill, recording the screen as you do so. Eventually, you should see and hear the more personable and likable you come through. At that point, of course, so will your listeners.

18

What to Do (and Think) at the Last Minute

Want to be sure you're a hit in your next online presentation? Here's what to do at the last minute for a successful performance!

If you're like most people, you worry about getting the content of your speech or presentation right. It's natural to be concerned that you won't leave out any essential information.

And that's fine—up to a point. In your planning and rehearsal, it makes sense to "check in" with yourself regularly to be sure you're getting in all the key points of your talk.

But kept up too long, focusing on presenting the content in exactly the right way can make you anxious. Worse, it can come between you and your primary purpose in a video meeting: getting everyone to grasp the true value of what you're saying. Think of it this way: the data you present and what all of it means to the group are two different things.

As in all of The Genard Method's techniques and approaches, the theater provides the perfect comparison. That is, worrying about the material too much is exactly the same situation actors face as they're about to go on stage. The lines they will be speaking are only the bare scaffold of their characters' inner lives and motivations, and, ultimately, the drama. So, whether you're acting or speaking virtually, what you do at the last minute before the "curtain" goes up is vital to your success.

The Body, The Mind, and Speaking Effectively

All of this concerns a question that as a speech coach I'm often asked: "What should I do just before I speak?" But it's as an actor that I can best answer it. That answer contains two parts: one concerned with the body, and the other with the mind.

Let's take the body first. Here, as ultimately in all things concerned with speaking, we have to start with the breath. Before you can consider anything having to do with a successful performance, you need to get yourself centered and poised. (We'll deal in a minute with what you should be thinking.)

Perhaps the most important element of effective performance is focus. And getting focused in the right way starts with breathing. Just ask any master who teaches yoga, meditation, or martial arts. In fact, actors have this saying: "If you're on top of your breathing, you'll be on top of your performance. And if you're not, you won't."

Your content helps get your message across. But it can't help you attain poise, presence, and the ability to connect with listeners. My advice, then, is to stop information cramming just before you speak, and pay attention to your breathing and "centering" yourself. In other words, put yourself in the right mode for communicating what you really want to say to the people on the other screens.

How to Influence Listeners

Now for the mental part of this powerful just-before-speaking routine. For this, let's take a peak backstage on opening night at the theater, where for the moment you're an actor about to go on.

You're standing in the wings, listening for the cue to make your entrance. Are you rehearsing your lines one last time to make sure you don't mess up in front of the audience?

Do that, and you might just freeze in front of these hundreds of people. If you don't know your lines by this point, you won't help yourself by trying to remember them now. For you, the right questions are: "What was I doing a moment ago?" "Where am I coming from as I enter this scene?" "What are my intentions here?" The answers to these questions aren't anywhere in your lines. They are part of the inner life of the character. Living them as you walk onstage gives the audience a real person, with motives and needs and desires.

Focus on people not information. Your situation as a speaker is much the same! You either know your content by now or you don't. If you spend time trying to remember how to say it exactly, you'll be on the wrong wavelength.

Just like the actor, your concern needs to be on your listeners: who they are, and what they need to hear. Most important: how can you get through to them concerning what you'll be saying?

Focusing this way makes you infinitely more valuable to the meeting than wrapping yourself in an information safety blanket. The needs of your listeners should always be front and center. The content of your talk serves that.

Interestingly, you won't lose one bit of the material you actually know well by now. And even if you do, you'll still be a presenter who is present and reaching the other participants. Isn't that better than someone who is anxious about delivering content perfectly?

19

Nervous at the Start of a Meeting? — This Helps!

Are nerves a problem at the start when you're presenting in an online meeting? Here's how to reduce anxiety in those first few critical moments.

If there's one problem we all share when speaking to a group, it's being just a little nervous at the start of a presentation. Does it make a difference if you're speaking live or in a virtual setting? Nope.

For some people, fear of public speaking

is even more serious than that. It may make them miserable, cause avoidance behavior, or even lead to changing careers! But even for the confident among us, the opening moments of a speech are challenging.

We may experience the Imposter Syndrome—which whispers to us, "It's only a matter of time before everyone realizes you don't know what you're talking about." Or we might experience the debilitating thought that we'll suddenly forget what we're supposed to say. We may even look at the faces on the screen in front of us and be horrified by how negative they all look. (They don't, we just imagine they do.)

Opening jitters like these aren't usually evidence of deep-seated speech anxiety. The "awful first two minutes" usually disappears once we get into our slides or comments. The problem is, listeners make judgments about us in the first 30-60 seconds. Waiting to get on track isn't much help if the judgment train has already left the station.

So, what can you do to derail this train of nerves?

You Already Know How to Be a Dynamic Speaker!

Recently, I worked with a client to get past her "Oh-my-God-how-do-I-start-out?" jitters. She is a high-performer at her company and well known in her industry. (I can almost hear her saying, as she thinks about her problem: "So what?")

Actually, the impetus for the "so what" shouldn't be an objection here, but a reason for confidence. And that's true for you too if you experience the Getting Started Blues. It all has to do with having faith in yourself. And I don't mean the religious kind.

The reason you get wrapped in anxiety when you're about to start a presentation is because you're over-focused on performance. Because you perform well in your job, you may think you have to be some kind of superhero at a professional presentation. Precisely because of your accomplishments, you believe people will think less of you if you don't perform at the level that's appropriate for your position.

But the meeting attendees aren't scoping out your performance at all. In fact, they couldn't care less. They're there to get something out of the session (especially if they're burdened with too many meetings to begin with!).

You, of course, have the goods: the insights that the slides or graphs can't deliver. As I tell clients, the thumb drive with your slide deck could have fallen out of your pocket earlier, and you could still nail your presentation.

After all, you've been asked to present this material for a reason. The reason is, you know what the information is about!

What does it matter, then, how smoothly you move through the slides?

In the end, you'll give the value expected of you because you're literally the only one who can do so. That's a pretty great reason for having faith in yourself, and not worrying that your opening is as smooth as glass.

When Memorization Can Help

Here's a practical way to make sure you hit the ground running: memorize the first minute of your talk. (And to seal the deal, do the same with your conclusion.)

In spite of some negative press, there are solid reasons why committing your intro to memory can help. For one thing, it keeps you from stumbling through your opening remarks. Since you'll only be committing a minute or so to memory, there's not much risk that you'll leave out anything.

Just as important: as I touched upon above, the first 60 seconds is critical to launching your speech successfully. Judgments about you—and decisions about whether to accept what you're saying—are formed during this period. That's why you need to grab listeners' attention and engage them right from the start.

Why not strut your best stuff when everyone is paying maximum attention? Show the audience they're in good hands. If the thought that you know exactly what you're going to say as you begin reduces your anxiety . . . well, it should!

20

Use Video to Get Better at Speaking Virtually

It was an amazing testament to the power of using video in presentation training. And it came when I least expected it.

As an actor and speech coach, I use video constantly to help my clients achieve greater presence as speakers. These days, of course, that means screen recordings of virtual sessions.

We all tend to be a little leery of seeing ourselves on video. I'm used to hearing clients say, "I don't want to see myself"—then invariably adding after they do: "It's not as bad as I thought!"

Video Shows You What Others See

But that day in one of The Genard Method's training rooms was different. The client was a father of the bride preparing for the traditional wedding reception toast. He was excited and apprehensive and wanted to help make the day special for the newlyweds, just like anyone would in his situation.

The fact that he had a neurological condition hadn't made a huge impression on me up until then. After all, he faced the same task everyone does who delivers a speech at a wedding, funeral, or special event: to speak to the best of his ability and reflect well on the occasion. That, then, was what I was working with him on.

It was his reaction to seeing himself after our first videotaping that caught me off guard. Continuous head nodding and shaking marked his condition. When he saw this on video, he was profoundly disturbed. I told him not to worry, that he couldn't do anything about his malady. But he said he would do something. He told me he would concentrate on keeping his head still for the entire five minutes of his toast.

And he did it! It was an extraordinary demonstration of the power of concentration. And it brought home to me—as dramatically as possible—just how valuable video can be in helping you prepare to speak.

Weddings are still being held, of course. But it's likely that you'll be speaking now in a webcast of some kind. The good news is that video remains as powerful a tool as ever for helping you prepare to speak at your best.

Below are four reasons why recording your practice sessions via video is one of the best decisions you can make.

1) Video Shows Your Energy Level

Most speakers focus on their content as they prepare to speak: "What am I going to say?" and, "How am I going to get it across?"

It's the second of those questions that bears serious thought as you prepare to speak. At this point, you're solid on your content; and your visuals are ready to go. What you should be thinking about now is how listeners will tune in—and turn on—to what you will say.

A big part of your success here depends upon the level of energy you bring to the screen.

I don't mean this just in a fuzzy, "Be energetic!" way. I'm talking about actual physics.

That renowned speech coach Sir Isaac Newton said it best:

"For every action, there's an equal and opposite reaction."

This means that if you give your audience an energetic performance, they will tend to respond more enthusiastically in return. But if your energy doesn't come through the screen (as it were), it will never cross the distance between everybody else's screen and their hearts and minds.

By screen-recording what the webcam sees, and watching it afterwards, you'll see where you score on the Speaker Energy Meter.

2) Video Helps You Stay Focused

"I look like I'm following a mouse with my eyes!" said my client. She happened to be a United States senator, and our coaching session was taking place inside the U.S. Capitol. And in this case, video was literally an eye-opener.

We were simulating an upcoming committee hearing, so the senator was sitting at a table speaking. One of her staffers videotaped our first take, and we watched it. That's when the senator saw what her eyes were doing while she was speaking. She meant that it looked as though she was following a mouse with her eyes as it ran around on the table.

We all chuckled at her remark, then got down to business. The video camera continued to tell the simple truth—which now was the senator's emerging ability to look at the witness with unwavering focus. As practiced speakers, politicians often have the talent to improve their outward demeanor quickly. But in this case, it was the video camera that provided the leverage.

3) Video Highlights Body Language

"I wander back and forth constantly."

"I seem to be swaying in an invisible breeze."

"I'm listing to starboard!"

Ask any speech coach, and they'll tell you they hear comments like these all the time from clients watching themselves on video. I call it having an out-of-body experience. Often for the first time, these speakers are seeing themselves as others do.

Because of this fairly magical ability, the camera teaches a powerful lesson: nonverbal communication can prevail over anything you say. So by all means, choose a great topic, and then practice as much as you have time for. But if you do something odd when others are watching you via video link, your credibility will dissolve quickly. Recording yourself will help you change that behavior before others have a chance to see it.

Remember, public speaking in all its forms is a performance art. Video shows how much of the 'physical you' contributes to the result.

Another true story. My client was a young professional in the financial industry who carried herself with poise and purpose. She had an important pitch coming up, and we were taping a practice session. Her command of the material was superb. That was clear on the video when we watched it afterward. But she was consumed with something else that she saw on the screen.

"Oh, my God!" she exclaimed. "Why am I rubbing my belly?!"

And she was right. For no reason other than habit, her right hand would rise from time to time, and start The Infamous Belly Rub.

Luckily, she saw this happening before her audience would notice it. Thanks, videotape.

4) Video Boosts Your Confidence

Now for the best news of all: video recordings—either with a camcorder or a webcam when speaking virtually—are definitely confidence boosters.

Yes, they will show you some things you'd rather not be aware of. But remember that in each case I mentioned above, viewing these behaviors led to solid improvement. The universal "It's not as bad as I thought!" reaction, in fact, usually leads to focused practice and growth.

The best aspect of video in this regard is what I call the Before-and-After Effect. Communication skills improvement is often hard to quantify. After all, it's not a case of "the software had a bug, but we found it."

Video can help fill the gap that comes from not having enough visible evidence. That's literally true, since it's all there in front of you! You might even have the response that many people do, when they see just how far they've come:

"Wow."

21

How to Develop a Stronger Online Presence

Are you a strong presence in video conferences? Here's how to talk to others with impact and influence.

It's a remote world now. The coronavirus has had all of us hunkered down for months. In some sectors, only a digital lifeline connects us with the rest of the world to conduct business.

Or so it seems.

It won't last, of course. And even now

amid the fear, the tragic loss of loved ones, and widespread economic destruction, we're surviving. More, we're learning. We're even innovating. Fortunately, interacting with colleagues, customers, and clients is "virtually" seamless via webcasts.

There's even more hope than that. Would you believe that all of those online meetings are helping you to develop stronger speaking presence?

Let's look at this striking paradox, one that's literally staring us in the face these days: remote communication is helping us to become more intimate.

Face-to-Face Communication: Still the Best!

It's actually part of another paradox that is shared by public speaking and the other world I inhabit: the theatrical stage. It's this: to have a relationship with a group, you need to sound like you're talking to individuals.

Watch an old newsreel of an orator from the late nineteenth or early twentieth century and you'll see exactly what I mean. We've gone from a bombastic style of speaking in public to one that is, well, to use the world I mentioned earlier, intimate.

These days, to connect with groups of strangers, you must appear to be just chatting as though you were in a conversation. (Of course, that's even truer if you're interacting virtually with your team.) The meeting may be a virtual one. But it's still face-to-face communication. The conversational speaking style is often hard for business speakers to adopt, because (they think) they're discussing serious issues.

This is where Zoom and the other video platforms come into their own. When you sit in front of your screen, you're actually much closer to each listener than you would be in a convention hall or even a conference room. The webcam places you just 18-24" inches away.

So you don't have to pull off the trick of being distant from audience members while trying to establish an emotional connection, the way you must do on a performance stage. You are close. Provided you open up enough emotionally, the other participants will experience you up-close and personal. That automatically lends you a stronger presence.

Time to Be Conversational

Online meetings, then, are giving you a powerful if often unrecognized tool. It's the capability— the insistence really—that you be conversational.

Every successful presentation sounds like the speaker is just talking to us. It's not speechifying in the old oratorical sense with one's finger in the air. Instead, it has the quality of a person-to-person chat.

There's a significant challenge here as well, however, which you must master for virtual speaking: how to externalize your emotions. It's something that actors spend their whole professional lives learning how to do. (As a poet once said, "An actor can break your heart at 50 feet.") And it's important in business as well, since all decisions have an emotional component.

You may think it's difficult to acquire this emotional openness. Chances are you haven't been trained in theatrical performance, which demands it. But the intimacy of the virtual environment makes it easier for you than if you were speaking from a big stage.

You're already close to us. Just lean in (literally), and don't be afraid of being intimate. The more you can make this whole thing feel like a close and friendly chat, the more present you'll be on our screens.

149

22

12 Ways to Prevent Employee Burnout

Your employees have carried your organization through a rough transition. They've gone above and beyond the call. Isn't it time to help keep them from burning out?

Are you amazed these days at your company's adaptability? Have you been impressed daily by how your team has thrown itself into the move to the virtual world?

Your leadership has been highly focused on how the organization can survive and thrive. Now it may be time to pay a little more attention to the people who continue to make that success possible.

As hard as the 2020 crisis has been on the bottom line, it's been just as tough on your loyal staff. According to one study, 75 percent of workers are experiencing burnout, and 40 percent say it's directly related to the pandemic.[8]

It's a double-whammy. First, there's the uncertainty, stress, and sheer physical threat of the coronavirus. Second, employees have had to learn new company procedures on the fly as everyone started working remotely.

Below are a dozen ways to show your staff how much you value them and care about their well-being. Cyberspace speeds

---

[8] https://www.flexjobs.com/blog/post/flexjobs-mha-mental-health-work-place-pandemic/

up everything, and burnout is no exception. So get moving now!

1. One of the easiest ways to head off virtual meeting burnout is to allow people to join by phone. Tell them they don't need to activate their video link. And let the team know that you really mean it. Some of my clients tell me that although the company allows this policy, nobody takes advantage of it because they're too scared. They don't want to be the first one to opt out of video.

2. Set priorities in terms of projects and assignments. It just makes sense. If people are spread too thin trying to work on a variety of projects, their contribution to each one will be diminished. Priorities also create the impression of crisp, clear thinking from leadership.

3. Give a small token of appreciation at frequent intervals. Gift cards (if possible, with some consideration of personal tastes) are ideal.

4. Allow your team members to choose

their own gift. Work with an employee recognition company that allows staff members to select their individual reward. An elegant gift box can work wonders!

5. Offer online exercise, yoga, or meditation classes. Or make it subscriptions to the wellness app of their choice.

6. Create the reverse of "work from home day" that used to delight employees but now makes them want to scream. Can you rent a facility for a day, where people can work at a safe distance while still collaborating? (Why not do this outside if the season is mild enough in your area?)

7. Throw in an extra mental health day per employee, one per month or every other month. Better yet, make it department-wide so that you don't hold a meeting where a key employee is missing.

8. Create a recipe board or healthy eating forum. Form an exercise club that people can join.

9. Set a reasonable rule for changes to scheduled meetings. If employees are scrambling to adjust their schedules at the last minute, they will rightly feel frazzled. It won't do much for their feeling of appreciation either.

10. Create boundaries. Encourage employees to physically separate their workspace from family space if they're working from home. Suggest that they dress for work, even if it's casual. Right now, they are missing the routines that used to be part of their professional lives. Help them establish a reasonable substitute.

Include temporal boundaries as well. The idea is for them to be able to turn off the clock when they don't need to be "on" for work. (Physical separation may be harder for them if they work from home, so setting a "time-divide" may be easier.) Establish a time when employees can be considered as officially off the clock. That means emails and work requests. If you're the head of the company, set an example. Don't cheat!

11. Avoid "adding on" to work loads. Don't give employees new assignments when they are already in the middle of a project.

12. Hold brainstorming meetings where creative ideas for working virtually can be shared. Make it clear that new ideas are welcomed, and people won't be penalized for them. If you can't create a safe environment for this to occur in your department or organization, skip it.

23

'Think on Your Seat': Two Exercises for Speaking Under Pressure

Whether you're virtually pitching an idea to the C-suite or rolling out new procedures for your team, you need to be able to think on your 'seat'. Here's how to up your game when the pressure is on!

Is there anything more sweat inducing than giving a high-profile presentation? That used to mean you'd be standing up in front of a group. Now, that group may be hundreds of viewers you're facing on a webcast.

Then there's always the possibility that your performance will be posted online and be there forever!

Even if you don't have fear of public speaking, important presentations have always tested your ability to handle pressure. In other words, to be able to think on your feet. Nowadays in virtual calls, you could say that you have to learn how to think on your seat.

Here are two exercises designed to help you survive the speech pressure cooker. Use one or the other (or both), based on the type of challenges you'll be facing.

Fast and Furious: "Quick-Writing" a Talk

You'll need a little lead-time for this one, though the actual exercise takes just fifteen minutes. Start by writing down the most challenging questions, examples of resistance, or objections you might face on an important topic in your work. (If you can make these jot-downs questions that you'd rather not be asked, great! — Better to stumble in this exercise than in a real video conference.) Put each one on a separate slip of paper.

Now put those slips of paper aside. If you can do this for a few days or a week, so much the better. The idea is to for you to forget what you wrote down. When you come back to your stash, you'll be facing those questions more or less the way you will in Q & A, i.e., on the spur of the moment. A variation of this part of the exercise is to have a colleague write the topics so you literally don't know what you're going to be asked.

When you're ready, and without looking, choose one item from the "hat." Now give yourself just fifteen minutes to compose a 2- to 3-minute response to that pressing question. Make sure you back up your assertions with evidence! You can speak from your notes.

Benefits of this exercise: This task tests four competencies: 1) your ability to organize a coherent response quickly; 2) your skill in marshaling evidence to strengthen a case; 3) your proficiency in constructing a logical argument; and 4) your dexterity in fashioning a credible response that gains buy-in from listeners.

If you're thinking that I'm being much too kind by giving you a whole 15 minutes to prepare . . . well, I admit it: I'm just a softie.

Turning Up the Heat: One-Minute Impromptus

Ready to really challenge yourself when it comes to thinking fast while still speaking eloquently? You can do so by practicing an exercise I call "One-Minute Impromptus."

The task here is straightforward but devilishly challenging. You'll have one minute to take notes on a topic a colleague gives you (or that you yourself have written down previously and have "forgotten about," per above). Then you'll immediately speak for one minute on that topic, again using your notes if need be. The timer on your smartphone will keep you honest.

Once again, the more you can relate the topic to your job and the resistance you face in online meetings, the better. When it comes to facing listeners who challenge you in this way, One-Minute Impromptus is a skills and confidence builder.

It may not seem that way at first. In fact, don't be surprised if the first time the timer beeps as you're speaking, you blurt out: "But I didn't get to the topic yet!"

In Round 2, you'll do better . . . so keep at it. Go through the exercise three, four, even five or six times in quick succession, building a mini-speech on a different topic each time. Screen-record all the sessions, and debrief your performance afterwards. You may be surprised at how quickly you improve your ability to speak intelligently and logically when you're under the gun.

Benefits of this exercise: One-Minute Impromptus tests your ability to be clear and concise and get to the heart of the matter. You're training yourself to speak with impact. If you really want to improve your ability to think on your seat, this is the exercise for you.

24

How to Handle Tough Questions and Pushback

Do you know your content but dread unexpected questions? Here's how to handle tough Q & A when it feels like you're the main online course!

Let's build on the previous chapter—where you practiced answering questions with little time to prepare. Now, we'll take a more strategic look at Q & A.

The way you respond to difficult questions in virtual engagements can change reality somewhat. For instance, you can give a terrific presentation that allows your online influence to soar. But it may come quickly crashing to earth if you can't answer legitimate questions or you sow confusion.

You might also face the following:

• Requests to go deeper into your points.

• Queries that have nothing whatever to do with your topic.

• Someone showing off.

• Outright hostility.

No, this isn't the time to leave town on a fast horse. But solid presentation prep requires thinking about how to succeed beforehand. That is, it's actually an opportunity for you to a) anticipate difficulties you may run into; b) show yourself off in a good light; c) maintain emotional control; and most important, d) strengthen your message and influence.

How do you accomplish all that? Simply follow the three steps below.

Step 1: Prepare Your Castle Before the Siege!

No self-respecting medieval mayor would allow his walled city to neglect stockpiling food, water, weapons, and supplies for a possible siege. Fortunately, your preparation can be more streamlined and straightforward (and involves fewer sharp weapons and large stones).

Actually, I use a metaphor along those lines with clients and trainees. When it comes to answering questions (I say), you can't be running around on the battlements dodging flaming arrows. The key is to establish control. To change metaphors: don't play defense. You have to score points—preferably a lot of them.

By all means, follow the standard advice about thinking ahead of time concerning the questions you'll be asked.

But don't turn yourself into a pretzel. I can testify from radio shows I've appeared on, that you will never anticipate some of the wacky questions you'll be asked. Spend time anticipating reasonable ones given your topic, then let it go.

You'll be much better served by being crystal clear about what your purpose is in this online presentation. I mean your specific purpose. To arrive at one, use an active infinitive verb concerning how you want your audience to respond.

Here are some examples: "I want to *inspire* these listeners . . . " "I have to *reassure* the employees . . . " "It's my job to *excite* the sales force about this new product," etc. Doing so will give you a huge advantage in terms of how you respond to questions.

The result of thinking this way is that everything you say in your responses will help achieve this purpose.

Here's a way to make this strategy even more actionable. Decide beforehand on the three, four, or five (no more) key points you want to get across in this meeting. If you routinely do this anyway, you'll be that much more ahead. You will use this strategy to . . .

Step 2: Turn Every Question to Your Advantage

This is how you transform a defensive bloodbath into a high score on your side of the board. You do so by using every opportunity in Q & A to get your critical points across, i.e., those 3-5 key points you decided on ahead of time.

Not every question will be meant to provoke or attack you, of course. But keep in mind that the following tactics work for all types of queries, whether hostile or not:

• **Reframe the Question.** This is a tactic that I teach diplomats at the U.S. State Department and the United Nations where I conduct training.

Many times, a question will be asked in a way designed to put you at a disadvantage. Sometimes, it will deliberately contain false information. In either of these cases, you should reframe the question in a way that a) is more accurate or fair, and b) prepares the ground so your answer is favorable to your side.

- **Set the Right Parameters.** Some questions are just too broad, or wholly outside the topic. When this is the case, let everyone know it right away. "I appreciate that question, but it's really beyond the scope of what I'm here to talk about" is a typical way you can begin.

This approach is also effective if you're in an interdepartmental meeting with people outside your department. Often, these are people with specialties in different disciplines than yours, such as lawyers, accountants, engineers, data scientists, etc. They understandably will ask about aspects of the project within their area of expertise.

But that may have to be dealt with in another meeting. That's a parameter you will have to be clear—and professional—in setting out for them.

- **Bridge to Your Key Points.** This is the tactic you see on display in political debates. Whether it's done cleanly or clumsily has entirely to do with the skill of the speaker.

The idea here is to get from what I call the boggy surface of an adverse question, over the bridge to the solid ground of your response. (Remember those key points you're using every opportunity to bring up!)

To be successful at bridging, keep two things in mind: (1) get across the bridge quickly, because every second you struggle in the bog means you're not making points. And (2) use different language to get the same message out.

The reason you say when you watch a debate, "S/he didn't answer a single question!" is because the candidate splashed around in the swamp before finally getting over the bridge. One thing that may have tipped you off: they kept saying the same thing using the identical language each time. How could you not spot the tactic? Avoid this trap by saying the same thing while using different words to do so.

Step 3: Maintain Emotional Control

Finally, when it comes to coping mechanisms for the worst kind of questions, emotional control is high on the list. Speaking of lists, I developed one that I call The 7 Danger Zones of Q & A. Here are these threats-in-question-form that you need to know about:

1. Hostile questions

2. Loaded questions

3. Leading questions

4. Hypothetical questions

5. Multifaceted questions

6. Fuzzy questions

7. False choices

Explaining each of these risky areas and appropriate strategies for each is beyond the scope of this chapter. Suffice to say: they all involve a response from you that is equal parts emotional equilibrium and poise.

These danger zones of agenda-based questions can easily make you feel attacked personally, rather than being questioned about your ideas. Naturally, you defend yourself.

But remember what I said earlier: your job is still to achieve your purpose in this encounter. When you get defensive, your purpose flies out the window.

So by all means defend yourself, but do so by advancing your position! That means, in part, always circling back to the points you're here to get across. Also, the moment you lose your cool you lose your audience. Let the other person alienate listeners.

A last piece of advice in terms of emotional control: breathe, and take your time. This is your talk, so take it at the pace you prefer. That not only keeps you on safer ground. It also makes you look like a leader, one who is in total control.

25

Giant Heads Are Staring at You: 7 Ways to Combat Zoom Fatigue

Whatever the post-pandemic future brings, we will do some of our work differently from now on. And more than ever, virtual tools will be at the center of our interactions. That means numerous online meetings every day. How can you save yourself and your team from the inevitable Zoom fatigue?

In 2020, March didn't come in like a lion or a lamb. It arrived with a new companion, named "Zoom fatigue."

No sooner were we relieved to learn that we could conduct business virtually, than we realized we were becoming exhausted. And unfortunately, it wasn't virtual exhaustion but the real thing. By April, the Harvard Business Review had featured an article on the new phenomenon. The following month, TED Ideas followed. Zoom fatigue was now an accepted mental and physical state that many of us were experiencing.

That didn't take long, did it?

What Causes Zoom Fatigue?

Remember a time when meeting virtually was refreshing, since you didn't have to drive across town or get on a plane? Why, then, are we now climbing the walls when we meet in virtual meetings at home instead of at the office?

There are a few very good answers to that question. For one thing, anything outside the norm is bound to be stressful. We're learning to be a new type of professional on the fly, using a technology that's fast overtaking the way we used to do our jobs.

Like any major change in our lives, that brings problems. We also have to proceed without the signposts that have helped us in the past in interpersonal communication. We especially miss the emotional clues that tell us how to navigate the shallows, shoals, or deep waters of conversations with others.

Also, our brains have to function differently, causing cognitive overload. Staring all day at a small screen means that our window on the world has been drastically reduced.

That means no interesting visual stimuli that used to break up meetings; no body language for us to observe; and nothing to see outside the window of the new room we're in. There isn't even anything in our peripheral vision that's different from what we've been seeing hour after hour!

In biological terms, we're also missing the rewards our brains usually receive from live face-to-face interactions.[9] No wonder we're feeling deprived!

What Can You Do?

Here are seven real fixes for this virtual conundrum.

1. Think about whether you actually need another virtual meeting. As an alternative, can you share a document online that people can give feedback on?

2. Consider a conference call instead. Or give team members the option to turn off their video feeds and participate only by audio.

3. De-tantalize your environment. Before a meeting begins, look around your workspace. What is there that's just dying

---

[9] 12. Redcay E, Dodell-Feder D, Pearrow MJ, et al. "Live face-to-face interaction during fMRI: A new tool for social cognitive neuroscience." Neuroimage. 2010; 50:1639-1647. Quoted in Jena Lee, "A Psychological Exploration of Zoom Fatigue," Psychiatric Times, July 27, 2020. Viewed at https://www.psychiatrictimes.com/view/psychological-exploration-zoom-fatigue

to pull your attention away from the screen during the upcoming meeting? It might be job-related or home-and-family related.

4. Give yourself mini-breaks. Look out the window. Close your eyes for a few seconds. Make an excuse to grab a work document so you have to stand up and move. And of course, try to give yourself a few minutes of downtime between meetings. And schedule time to eat!

5. Switch from speaker view to gallery view to thumbnail view, and back again. You'll literally see everybody differently.

6. Hide Thyself. One source of stress in virtual meetings is that we look at ourselves too much. Once we do, we become focused on how we look to others. Right-click on your video image in Zoom, click on the ellipses (those three horizontal dots), and chose "Hide Myself."

7. Take a brief time before you join a meeting to calm and center yourself. Close your eyes, breathe, and locate yourself

in your body and in the room. Smile slightly. Now open your eyes and join the conversation.

* And thanks to TED Ideas for the "Giant Heads" part of the title of this chapter.

Interested in an .mp3 audio recording that will help you relax? It's my "Time to Relax: The Progressive Relaxation Exercise," narrated by me. Find it in the store at www.genardmethod.com.

Share Your Ideas and Best Practices!

Want others to know about your successful tips, hacks, and solutions for online meetings? We're all learning every day about how to excel in the virtual environment. Let's do this together!

If you'd like to share your experience (either individually or as a team) in online meetings, video conferences, or webinars, please tell me about them at:

info@genardmethod.com

It will be interesting to keep the conversation going with readers' experiences (yours) to the evolving world of doing business virtually. I'd be delighted to hear from you.

The Genard Method

The Genard Method is a unique system of communication skills training based in the techniques of the theater. Developed by stage actor and executive speech coach, Dr. Gary Genard, the Method helps executives and teams access their natural talents to speak for leadership.

Great speakers use emotions and performance skills—not just information—to bring their ideas to life. Like them, you will discover how to be a more memorable speaker who positively influences audiences of all kinds. Perhaps you will become exceptional—or even extraordinary.

Clients and trainees of the Method learn how to speak with excellence in any professional situation. Techniques include message development, storytelling, voice improvement, body language, in-person and online presence, commanding a stage, virtual speaking skills, and developing a keen sense of audience psychology and persuasion. Dr. Genard's programs are designed to empower anyone to reach their highest personal level of speaking excellence.

To learn more about how The Genard Method can help you, your group, or your leadership team speak with absolute poise and professionalism, please visit:

www.GenardMethod.com

The **Genard** Method

93 Concord Avenue

Belmont, MA 02478

(617) 993-3410

+1-617-993-3410

www.GenardMethod.com

info@genardmethod.com

Speak at Your Best Professionally!

Books by Dr. Gary Genard

Whether you're starting out or a seasoned pro, discover the performance secrets of speaking with power and presence.

- Build your confidence, poise, and professionalism.
- Engage audiences while moving them to action.
- Improve your vocal skills for the sound of leadership.
- Command any stage—in person or virtually!

Get these books on The Genard Method, from one of America's leading speech coaches:

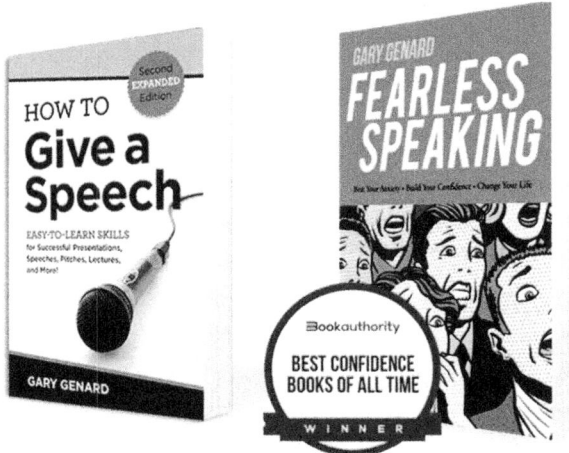

www.genardmethod.com

Made in the USA
Monee, IL
12 September 2021